American Humane.

Protecting
Children & Animals
Since 1877

American Humane Pet Care Library

Hamsters, Gerbils, Guinea Pigs, Rabbits, Ferrets, Mice, and Rats

How to Choose and Care for a Small Mammal

Laura S. Jeffrey

Enslow Publishers, Inc.

40 Industrial Road   PO Box 38
Box 398   Aldershot
Berkeley Heights, NJ 07922   Hants GU12 6BP
USA   UK

http://www.enslow.com

American Humane.

Protecting
Children & Animals
Since 1877

The American Humane Association is dedicated to preventing the cruelty, abuse, neglect, and exploitation of children and animals. To learn how you can support the vision of a nation where no child or animal will ever be a victim of willful abuse or neglect, visit www.americanhumane.org, phone (303) 792-9900, or write American Humane at 63 Inverness Drive East, Englewood, Colorado, 80112-5117.

Library of Congress Cataloging-in-Publication Data

Jeffrey, Laura S.
    Hamsters, gerbils, guinea pigs, rabbits, ferrets, mice, and rats : how to choose
      and care for a small mammal / Laura S. Jeffrey.
      p. cm. — (American humane pet care library)
    Summary: Explains the different personalities of several small mammals, where to
      go to pick the right one, and how to keep them happy and healthy.
    Includes bibliographical references and index.
    ISBN 0-7660-2518-7
    1. Pets—Juvenile literature. 2. Mammals—Juvenile literature. [1. Mammals. 2. Pets.] I. Title.
    SF416.2.J46 2004
    636.088'7—dc22

                       2003022969

Printed in the United States of America

10 9 8 7 6 5 4 3 2

To Our Readers: We have done our best to make sure all Internet Addresses in this book were active and appropriate when we went to press. However, the author and the publisher have no control over and assume no liability for the material available on those Internet sites or on other Web sites they may link to. Any comments or suggestions can be sent by e-mail to comments@enslow.com or to the address on the back cover.

Every effort has been made to locate all copyright holders of material used in this book. If any errors or omissions have occurred, corrections will be made in future editions of this book.

Illustration Credits: © 1996–2004 ArtToday, Inc., pp. 7 (left), 9 (left), 17 (right), 28, 35 (left and right), 39 (top), 41 (right); John Bavaro, pp. 44, 45; Corel Corporation, pp. 7 (right), 37 (left); EyeWire, pp. 29, 34, 40; Hemera Technologies, Inc. 1997–2000, pp. 5 (left), 14, 15, 19, 22, 27, 33; Painet, Inc., pp. 5 (right), 9 (right), 13, 16, 42; PhotoDisc, Inc., pp. 1, 8, 11, 12, 23, 31, 36, 37 (right), 38, 39 (bottom); © 2002 PIXTAL, pp. 3, 4, 6, 10, 17 (left), 18, 21, 24, 25, 26, 30, 41 (left), 43.

Cover Illustration: Corel Corporation (Horse); PhotoDisc, Inc. (Gerbil, Dog, Fish, Cat, Bird).

Contents

Rabbits are just one kind of small mammal.

Great Pets

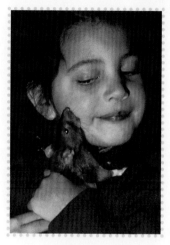

 Small mammals such as mice, rats, hamsters, gerbils, guinea pigs, rabbits, and ferrets make great pets. Unlike cats and dogs, small mammals can fit into almost any room in any house. They do not need constant attention, so they are good pets for families who are often away during the day.

This book will help you choose the right small mammal for you. It will tell you what to feed your new pet and how to make it feel comfortable and safe. You will learn how to keep your new pet healthy and happy.

Not many people think of rats as pets, but they are smart and can be trained.

Small mammals can live anywhere from two to ten years with proper care.

The History of Small Mammals

Compared with other animals, small mammals do not have a long history as pets. For example, dogs and cats have been pets for thousands of years. But it was really not until the twentieth century that small mammals became household pets. Hamsters came to the United States in 1938. Before that time, they were used in Israel, France, and England for medical research.

Rabbits are believed to be the third most common pet in the United States.

Small mammals have become very popular pets. In fact, rabbits are believed to be the most common pet today after cats and dogs.

Ferrets are also becoming popular pets. In some areas, however, they are illegal. Or, you may need a license to have a ferret. Before bringing a ferret into your home, call your local wildlife department, fish and game department, or animal welfare agency. Find out if you are allowed to keep a ferret as a pet.

Most small mammals live anywhere from two to ten years. With proper care, they will give their owners love and friendship for many years.

Ferrets are becoming popular pets.

The Right Pet for You

There are many different kinds of small mammals. Each type has its own needs, and each behaves in a certain way. It is important to pick a pet that matches your lifestyle.

Each type of small mammal needs special care and attention.

Mice and Rats

Many people are surprised to learn that mice and rats make terrific pets. Mice that are handled regularly become very gentle. Rats are very smart. They can be taught to respond to their

With regular handling and care, mice and rats can become very gentle.

owner's voice and touch. They also respond to food rewards.

Hamsters

Hamsters are clean and odorless. But they like to sleep during the day and stay up all night. They are also known to get upset easily, and they may bite or nip at their owners. Because of this, hamsters may not be the best small mammal for you.

Gerbils

Gerbils are gentle and curious. They become lonely when they are not around other gerbils. In some areas, gerbils are illegal. If you choose this small mammal, you should get two. Just make sure the two you choose are both male or both female.

Guinea pigs come in many different colors.

Guinea Pigs

A guinea pig may also be known as cavy (rhymes with navy). They come in many breeds and colors. The three basic types are shorthaired, longhaired, and medium-length or swirl-coated. Guinea pigs learn to

recognize their owners. They will greet a favorite person with loud whistles and squeaks. They are very social animals, so if you have room, get two.

Rabbits

Rabbits also come in many breeds. They are loyal, affectionate pets. They are also very playful and enjoyable to be around.

Ferrets

Many people find ferrets to be lovable pets. Ferrets have a lot of energy and are curious. Owners must be willing to pay extra time and attention to this pet. Ferrets are very social animals. They may get along well in houses with dogs and cats. Ferrets can even be trained to do tricks.

When you get your new pet, check to make sure its coat is shiny and healthy.

Learn More

You can learn more about the different kinds of small mammals by exploring Web sites on the Internet or visiting your local library. You can also call a humane society.

Once you have decided which small mammal to get, check with your local animal welfare agency. They may have small mammals that you could adopt. If they do not, ask your veterinarian to give you the name of a good breeder. A vet may also know people who are looking to find a new home for their own pets. Do not get your new pet from the wild. Wild animals do not make good pets.

Ferrets make unique and interesting pets.

Wherever you go to get your new pet, take your time and look around. The cage and the animal should be clean. The animal should be active and alert. If it is asleep, ask to have it awakened. Then, watch the animal move around.

The animal should not show any signs of poor health. These signs include not moving around, sneezing, scratching, discharge from the eyes or nose, bald spots, untreated injuries, a soiled area on or under the tail, or soft feces.

Animals should not have parasites such as ear mites, worms, and maggots. Check the animal's bedding or droppings for parasites, too. Make sure the animal does not have crusty spots on the inside of its ears.

Fast Fact

Rats are very smart. They can be trained with food to come when their name is called.

Many people who are allergic to cats and dogs are also allergic to rabbits and guinea pigs. These small mammals can shed heavily during certain times of the year. You may want to be tested for allergies before bringing any small mammal into your home.

Pet Pointer

Think twice, if you are adopting a small mammal because you are allergic to cats or dogs.

15

Set up your new pet's home before you bring it home.

Taking Care of Your New Pet

No matter which small mammal you choose, set up its housing before you bring it home. Avoid placing the housing in direct sunlight or in drafty areas. Your animal's house should be in its own quiet area of your home. Make sure the housing you select for your pet is secure. Avoid plastic housings because they can be chewed and your pet might escape.

The housing you choose for your new pet should be the proper size.

Mice and Rats

Mice and rats can be housed in either a big glass aquarium with a screened top or a solid-bottom cage with a wire top. To prevent any injuries to your pet's feet, make sure that most of the bottom of the cage is covered with solid flooring.

The floor of the cage should be covered with solid flooring so your pet will not hurt its feet.

Because rats are so smart, they usually will find a way out of their cage unless you secure it properly. If you have a wire cage, make sure the openings are not wide enough for your rat to squeeze through. The screened top should be weighted.

Inside the cage, put in ladders, tunnels, and safe toys for your pet to explore and enjoy. You should also add a fully enclosed nesting box. This box should be about five inches square with a small entrance. The entrance should be one inch for mice and two inches for rats.

This nesting box can be as simple as a cardboard box. When the box becomes chewed or soiled, replace it.

Always place a few pieces of hardwood in the cage. Gnawing on the hardwood will help your pet wear down its always growing teeth.

The floor of the cage should be covered with shredded newspaper, kitty litter, peat moss, hay,

Fast Fact

Certain foods such as cake and crackers can get stuck in a hamster's cheek pouches and cause eye infections.

or straw. This layer should be at least one inch deep so your pet can burrow. Mice and rats are very curious, so give them toys. They like to explore boxes and to chew on and crawl through cardboard tubes.

Avoid wire exercise wheels because they pinch tails. A solid plastic wheel or runabout ball are safer choices.

Use a water bottle that is the right size for your pet. Change the water daily.

Feed your mice or rats food that will keep them healthy. A nut/seed mix is the perfect mixture. You can occasionally treat them to dried fruit slices, fiesta-type mixes, crackers, rolled oats, plain croutons, alfalfa hay, fresh fruits, dry cooked rice, and raisins. Remove any uneaten or spoiled food or your pet may want to hoard it.

Hamsters

A big glass aquarium with a screened top or a solid-bottom cage with a wire top is also a good home for a hamster. Unlike many animals, adult hamsters do not like company. They like to live alone, so keep only one hamster. Adult hamsters have been known to hurt or even kill their roommates.

Hamsters are also known for escaping from their cage. If this happens, place your pet's cage in the middle of the room with the door open and fresh food inside. In the morning, you may find that the hamster returned during the night and is now sleeping happily.

For bedding, hamsters prefer shredded paper, cat litter, peat moss, hay, or straw. You should also give them chew sticks and a nesting box.

Hamsters enjoy special hamster food. Feed your pet in the evening, and sometimes add vegetables or other fresh foods. Hamsters love

Your new pet will need something to chew on to keep its teeth and gums healthy.

to burrow. To burrow is to dig a hole or tunnel in the bedding and hide in it. Hamsters are also hoarders, filling their cheek pouches with food and then scurrying away to hide their treasure.

Fast Fact

The teeth of all small mammals grow continuously. Your pet needs an unpainted and untreated piece of hardwood to chew on so it can keep its teeth short.

Gerbils

Gerbils need a cage with plenty of room to burrow, nest, exercise, and leap. Buy a cage with lots of shelves, levels, and connecting tunnels. Give your pet lots of toys such as paper rolls, branches, and cardboard boxes. Cover the floor of the cage with a thick layer of paper, which your pet will love to shred. You can also use unscented cat litter or sand.

Like hamsters, gerbils burrow. They also thump. For unknown reasons, every few days, gerbils go to a corner of their cage and thump their hind limbs. They are also great leapers and have earned the nickname "kangaroo rats." So make sure to securely cover the top of the cage.

Feed your gerbils specially prepared food mixture in the evening, when your pets are more active. Occasionally, treat your pets to dates, carrots, or alfalfa.

Guinea Pigs

An ideal home for a guinea pig is a galvanized wire cage. Cover the bottom with a sturdy carpet scrap or other solid flooring that can be easily replaced.

Hamsters like to hoard their food. They will fill their cheeks with food, and then hide it.

The best type of bedding for guinea pigs is a layer of hay or straw on top of a layer of peat moss. Hardwood blocks such as chew toys help wear down their teeth.

Guinea pigs eat often, so give them plenty of specially prepared guinea pig pellets. They also enjoy "greens" such as carrots, apples, timothy hay, and even fresh slices of orange. Do not give rabbit pellets to your guinea pig. Rabbit food does not have Vitamin C, which a guinea pig needs.

Guinea pigs need plenty of room in their cage to burrow, nest, exercise, and leap.

Guinea pigs need to be groomed. They also have long nails that must be carefully trimmed every few weeks. Ask your veterinarian for help with this delicate task.

Guinea pigs need lots of room for exercise, or they will become obese. If possible, let your pet out of its cage in a closed room.

Rabbits

The best home for a rabbit is a galvanized wire cage made especially for rabbits. The cage you buy should be at least four times bigger than the size of the rabbit. If you are getting a young rabbit, make sure the cage will be four times larger than the rabbit when it is full grown.

Guinea pigs need to be groomed. Their nails also need to be trimmed every few weeks.

Partially cover the cage floor with cardboard or a sisal mat.

For bedding in the cage, place a thick layer of hay or straw on top of a layer of peat moss. Do not use sawdust because the dust can harm the rabbit's breathing system. Give your rabbit an enclosed sleeping box. The entrance should be at the top of one side.

You should not house your rabbit outside. Outdoor housing attracts flies that can make your rabbit sick. Outdoor rabbits may get heat stress in the summer and frostbite in the winter. Also, the rabbit's water might freeze in the winter.

Make sure your rabbit's cage will be big enough when it is full grown.

Your rabbit could also be attacked by other animals.

The best diet for your rabbit is rabbit pellets. You can also give your rabbit alfalfa hay and a salt block. Some fresh vegetables can make your rabbit ill, so check with a vet, animal shelter, or other expert for advice. Rabbits, like other small mammals, need fresh water, changed every day. Rabbits can sometimes misbehave, so make sure the food and water bowls are too heavy for your pet to knock over.

Some people train their rabbits to use a litter box. They also let their pet roam inside—after rabbit-proofing the home, of course. Make sure no loose dogs, cats, or other pets will threaten the safety of your rabbit.

Fast Fact

You can give your rabbit carrots and apples.

Pay special attention to your rabbit's toenails. They may need to be trimmed by a veterinarian because they grow rapidly. To prevent overgrown teeth, give your rabbit hay, straw, and blocks made of hardwoods to chew.

Rabbits need regular, supervised exercise outside of their cage to stay healthy and happy. Make sure your pet does not chew on electrical cords during its indoor outings. Unlike many other small mammals, a rabbit should have the opportunity to spend much of its awake time out of the cage. Rabbits require a larger area to exercise and play in.

To avoid behavioral and health problems, pet rabbits should be spayed or neutered. If you get your rabbit from an animal shelter

Fast Fact

Gerbils enjoy having their backs and ears scratched gently.

Rabbits need regular exercise outside their cage. Make sure you keep an eye on your pet.

or rescue agency, this may have already been done for you.

Ferrets

Ferrets should be housed in cages large enough to hold a litter box, nesting and sleeping area, and toys. This usually amounts to a space that is fourteen inches wide by twenty-four inches long and ten inches high. Of course, this space can be bigger if you have the room.

Ferrets should be housed in a cage that is large enough for a litter box, nesting and sleeping area, and toys.

Ferrets do not like temperatures above 95 degrees Fahrenheit, so do not place their cage in direct sunlight.

For nesting and sleeping, ferrets enjoy a soft cloth, old T-shirt, or a towel. The nesting and sleeping area should be placed in the opposite corner from the litter box. When giving your ferret toys, keep in mind that you should not give it anything it can swallow.

Ferrets are carnivores. That means they are meat eaters. They enjoy a diet of specially prepared food or cat food that is high in animal protein. Young ferrets, called kits, and old ferrets need special diets. Young ferrets should be fed a cup of food a day that has water added to it. Allow the food to soak in the water for ten or fifteen minutes before giving it to your pet.

Older ferrets have problems digesting the protein in their food, so you should add 1/2 teaspoon of vegetable oil to it. Avoid feeding your ferret any dairy or sugar products. They can be harmful.

Since ferrets have a lot of energy and are smart, be sure their food dishes are weighted so they cannot be tipped over. Also, be sure to place these dishes near the nesting area and not their litter box.

Ferrets are smart and curious creatures. Be sure to watch your pet carefully when you take it out of the cage.

You should also let your ferret roam outside its cage regularly. Ferrets have a lot of energy and need to run and explore outside of the cage every day. Just make sure to supervise your pet to keep it safe and prevent it from becoming destructive.

Your ferret will sometimes need a bath and nail trimming. For bathing, use a tearless baby shampoo or one made just for ferrets. Your ferret will need to be bathed only once every few months. Bathing it too much can bother a ferret's skin and cause its coat to become dull.

Ferrets, like dogs and cats, will need vaccinations, and should be spayed or neutered to avoid health and behavior problems.

Things to Know

No matter which kind of small mammal you choose as a pet, make sure you clean its cage regularly. Every week, wash the entire cage with hot, soapy water. Use only liquid dishwashing soap. Rinse the cage and then dry it well before putting your pet back. After the cage is clean and dry, replace your pet's bedding. Do not use wood shavings such as pine and cedar. They contain chemicals that can harm your pet.

All cage equipment, such as water bottles

Fast Fact

Place your pet's cage out of direct sunlight but where there is something to look at, such as a fish tank or fish bowl.

and food bowls, should be cleaned with watered-down bleach water (for example, one tablespoon of bleach in one gallon of water) once a week. This stops bacteria buildup.

If you are training your pet to use a litter box, do not use clay, clumping sand, cat litter, or corncob litters. These are harmful to small animals if swallowed. Instead, use plain (without print or ink) paper pulp, dry grass pellets, aspen wood shavings or compressed sawdust pellets.

No matter which small mammal you get for a pet, take good care of it.

Always wash your hands before handling your pet. You may have traces of food, salt, or sugar on your skin that may cause the animal to bite. Make sure to wash your hands afterward as well.

5

Healthy and Happy

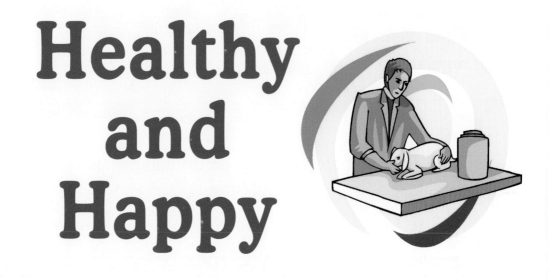

 A veterinarian is a doctor who takes care of sick and injured animals. A vet also makes sure animals stay healthy. There are no vaccinations for most small mammals. But a vet will be able to tell you if your pet is in good health. You may even want to take a small mammal to the vet for a checkup before you decide to take it home. A vet can also answer any questions you might have.

A vet will make sure your small mammal stays healthy.

35

To keep your pet healthy, feed it the correct food, make sure it has clean water, and clean its cage regularly.

_____

If your pet stops eating or drinking or is less active than normal, call the vet. You should also call if your pet is having trouble breathing, is not having bowel movements or is having diarrhea, or is having problems performing simple tasks.

Ferrets do need annual visits to the vet. They should get a checkup and a shot called a distemper booster. Distemper is a disease. The booster gives your pet extra protection against the disease. Ferrets, especially females, are likely to get tumors and ulcers. Watch your ferret's behavior. Call the vet right away if your ferret acts lethargic, which means it does not seem to have any energy. Also call the vet if your pet is not eating or drinking.

6

Preventing Problems

Most small mammals bite if they are frightened or angry. So you should get your pet comfortable with being held. To pick up your mouse or rat, gently close your hand around it. Lift it by the base of the tail with one hand while slipping your other hand under its body. Never squeeze or pick up a mouse or rat by the tail, midsection, or base of the neck.

Learn to pick up your pet properly. Hamsters become nervous when they are held in a cupped hand. So hold your pet by gently grasping the

Learn the proper way to pick up your new pet.

Gerbils do not usually bite and enjoy being held.

loose skin on the back of its neck while your other hand is under it. Never pick it up by just the neck, and always keep your hand under it.

Because of their friendly nature, gerbils do not usually bite. They enjoy being handled. In fact, the more you handle them, the better they like people. To pick up a gerbil, scoop it onto your open palm. You also can pick it up by the base of the tail. Do not pick it up by the tip of the tail because that part is very fragile.

When handling a guinea pig, never pick it up by its scruff, which is the hair on its neck. Gently cradle your pet in one hand while securing its body with the other hand.

Learning to lift your rabbit requires time and patience. One thing to keep in mind is that you must always hold your rabbit snugly against your body. One way to hold a rabbit is called the "chest-to-chest" hold. This means carrying the rabbit vertically (up and down) against your chest with its head near yours. Another way to carry it is called the "football hold." This means holding the rabbit with its rump in one of your hands and its head in the crook, or bend, of your elbow.

Be patient when learning to pick up your rabbit.

Ferrets should be picked up with two hands.

Ferrets should be picked up using two hands. One of your hands should support its chest, and the other should support its hips.

You and Your New Pet

 After you bring a small mammal into your home, you will be happy to spend time with it there. You can learn more about your pet by logging on to the Internet, with an adult's permission. There, you will find a lot of information. You might also want to join a "virtual community" of others your age who have the same kind of pet.

Small mammals can make great pets.

41

Small mammals make great pets. Once you bring your new pet home, you will have fun taking care of it.

Keep loving and learning more about your pet. Then you and your mice, rats, hamsters, gerbils, guinea pigs, rabbits, or ferrets can spend many happy years together.

Learn more about your new pet by visiting your library or logging onto the Internet.

1.

When hamsters are born, their eyes are closed and they do not have any hair.

2.

After a few weeks, baby hamsters begin to grow hair and their eyes start to open.

44

3.

A full-grown hamster can live between two and four years with the proper care.

Words to Know

burrow—To dig a hole or a tunnel in bedding and hide in it.

galvanized—Made of a metal specially coated to prevent rust.

hoard—To hide food to eat at a later time.

lethargic—Sleepy, without energy.

mammals—Warm-blooded animals whose babies feed on their mother's milk.

neuter—To operate on a male animal so that it cannot reproduce. This operation prevents overpopulation.

sisal—A strong fiber used to make rope and other items.

spay—To operate on a female animal so that it cannot reproduce. This operation prevents overpopulation.

vaccination—A shot that prevents disease.

Learn More About Small Mammals

Books

Gelman, Amy. *My Pet Ferrets*. Minneapolis, Minn.: Lerner Publications, Co., 2001.

Head, Honor. *Rats & Mice*. Austin, Tex.: Raintree Steck-Vaughn, 2001.

Hinds, Kathryn. *Hamsters and Gerbils*. New York: Benchmark Books, 2001.

Holub, Joan. *Why Do Rabbits Hop?: And Other Questions About Rabbits, Guinea Pigs, Hamsters, and Gerbils*. New York: Dial Books for Young Readers, 2003.

Internet Addresses

Animaland
<http://www.animaland.org>
Click on Pet Care for more information about the care of different pets.

Just For Kids
<http://www.americanhumane.org/kids/index.html>
Find out more about pets on this site from the American Humane Association.

47

Index

A
adoption, 13
allergies, 15
animal welfare agency, 8, 13
aquarium, 18, 20

B
bald spots, 14
bathing, 32
burrowing, 20, 22, 23, 24

C
carnivores, 31
cavy, 11
"chest-to-chest," 39

D
distemper, 36

E
ear mites, 14
exercise, 22, 24, 25, 28, 29

F
ferrets, 5, 8, 12, 13, 29–32, 36, 40, 43
"football hold," 39
frostbite, 26

G
gerbils, 5, 11, 22, 23, 28, 38, 43
gnawing, 19
guinea pigs, 5, 11–12, 15, 23–25, 39, 43

H
hamsters, 5, 7, 10–11, 19, 20–22, 23, 37–38, 43, 44, 45
hardwood, 19, 22, 24, 28
heat stress, 26
housing, 17

K
"kangaroo rats," 23
kits, 31

L
license, 8
litter box, 27, 29, 30, 31, 33

M
maggots, 14
mice, 5, 9–10, 18–20, 37, 43

N
nails, 25

nesting box, 19, 21
neutering, 28, 32

P
parasites, 14

R
rabbits, 4, 5, 7, 8, 12, 15, 25–29, 39, 43
rats, 5, 9–10, 14, 18–20, 37, 43

S
scratching, 14
sisal mat, 26
sleeping box, 26
spaying, 28, 32

T
toenails, 28
tumors, 36

U
ulcers, 36

V
vaccinations, 35
veterinarian, 25, 27, 28, 35, 36

W
worms, 14

48